The Lost Village of Skara Brae

Contents

Written by Mick Gowar and Sarah-Jane Harknett

Illustrated by Philip Bannister

Collins

The lost village

The village of Skara Brae is more than 4,000 years old. It was built on the biggest island of the **Orkneys** in a time which **archaeologists** call the **New Stone Age**. The people who lived then made tools like knives and axes from stone, usually **flint**.

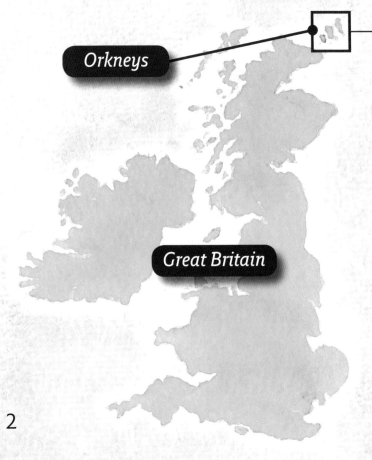

Orkneys

Great Britain

People lived together in small villages and grew crops like barley and wheat, and kept animals. Skara Brae was buried for over 4,000 years under tonnes of sand and soil, and wasn't found again until 1850.

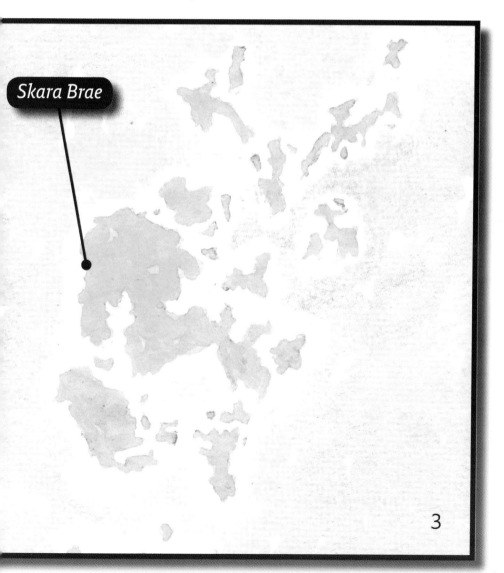

Skara Brae

The Great Storm, 1850

In the winter of 1850 fierce storms battered the British Isles. Two hundred people living near the coast were drowned. Huge waves crashed on to the coast of the Bay of Skaill.

What was found

Tonnes of sand and soil were washed away,
or blown away by the strong winds.
The storm uncovered the remains of
stone walls. Sir William Watt, who owned
the land, and some of his farm workers
started to dig around the walls.

Digging carried on for 18 years during the short summer months. Four stone houses were found, complete apart from their roofs. Beds, fireplaces and shelves – all made of stone – were also found inside the houses.

Small **finds** like pots, tools and necklaces were taken to Sir William's home, although now they are kept in museums.

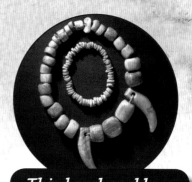

This bead necklace was found in one of the houses.

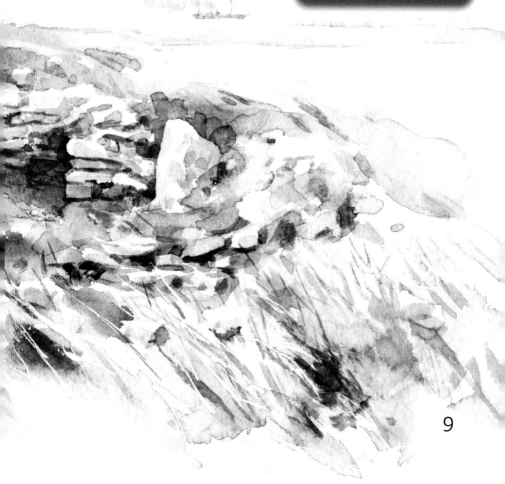

9

Another storm and more finds

In 1925 Orkney was struck by another great storm. More sand and soil were washed away by the huge waves and strong winds. Some of the houses at Skara Brae were damaged, but the remains of other houses were uncovered.

Between 1928 and 1930, archaeologists found another four buildings, linked to the original houses by paths.

Inside the houses they also found knife-blades made of stone, and pins and beads made of bone. These things show us what tools the people who lived in the village used, and how they fastened and decorated their clothes.

This stone knife would have been used to cut meat or wood.

The village then

The houses were so well **preserved** that we can easily imagine what the village might have looked like more than 4,000 years ago.

workshop

making tools from flint

house

Up to 20 families would have lived in
Skara Brae.

How they lived

We know what the villagers would have eaten from the tools, bones and shells that have been found.

> *The villagers would have kept pigs and cattle.*

hunting deer for meat and skins

fishing, and collecting shellfish to eat

Today, visitors to Orkney can see how a house might have looked.

The original roof has rotted away. A new one, made from wood and whale's ribs covered with moss, has been placed over the one room.

beds filled with **bracken** to make a mattress

blankets made from animal skins

Copies of the villagers' most precious objects – beads, pins and pots – have been placed on the stone **dresser**. Animal skin curtains have been hung around the stone bed.

bead necklace, bracelet, and pins made from **walrus** tusks

fireplace

Modern Orkneys

Today, over 19,000 people live on the islands, and their way of life is very different from the way people lived in the New Stone Age. Farming is still important, especially beef farming, but there is also an oil terminal, and the most up-to-date **plant** in Britain for making electricity from **wave power**.

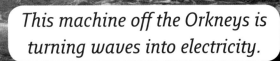

This machine off the Orkneys is turning waves into electricity.

But Orkney's past is important too, and many
people come to see Skara Brae and the other
world famous sites in the Orkneys. They help
modern visitors understand what life was like
5,000 years ago.

Glossary

archaeologists	people who learn about the past by studying objects that have been dug up
bracken	a fern-like plant
dresser	a set of shelves for storing dishes, etc.
finds	objects found by archaeologists that can tell them about the past
flint	a type of stone that can be sharpened to make simple tools
New Stone Age	a time in history when people used stone to make tools. It began about 11,000 years ago and ended about 4,000 years ago.
Orkneys	a group of 70 islands off the north coast of Scotland
plant	a factory
preserved	kept as they were
walrus	an animal like a seal, but much bigger and with very long tusks. It lives in the sea and on beaches.
wave power	electricity that is created from the movement of the sea

Index

Skara Brae through time

1850
the Great Storm

4,000 years ago
life at Skara Brae

1850-51
the first dig

1925
the second storm

now
one house rebuilt

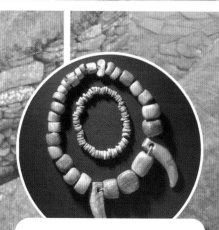

1928-30
the second dig

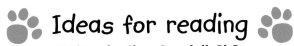

Ideas for reading

Written by Clare Dowdall, PhD
Lecturer and Primary Literacy Consultant

Reading objectives:
- predict what might happen on the basis of what has been read so far
- listen to and discuss a wide range of non-fiction
- make inferences on the basis of what is being said and done

Spoken language objectives:
- use spoken language to develop understanding through speculating, imagining and exploring ideas
- give well-structured descriptions, explanations and narratives for different purposes
- maintain attention and participate actively in collaborative conversations

Curriculum links: History

Interest words: archaeologists, dresser, finds, flint, New Stone Age, Orkneys, plant, preserved, walrus, wave power

Word count: 528

Resources: atlas/image of the British Isles on whiteboard

Build a context for reading

- Using an atlas, or an image of the British Isles, identify England, Ireland, Scotland and Wales and draw children's attention to the Orkney Islands. Explain that they will be reading about a village on Orkney in an information book.

- Show children the front cover. Read the title and blurb with them and help the children to pronounce *Skara Brae*. Explain that this is the name of the village. Ask children to predict how the village was "lost". Discuss what a village is, and their own experiences.

- Ask children to use the contents to find the glossary. Discuss what the glossary is used for. Using the words *archaeologists* and *preserved* remind children of some strategies for tackling longer unfamiliar words, e.g. using phonic strategies, looking for words within words, breaking the word into syllables before blending, looking for familiar word endings.

Understand and apply reading strategies

- Turn to pp2–3. Read this aloud with the children. If children have learnt about other ancient civilisations, compare the information provided about the New Stone Age to these, e.g. Romans, Egyptians.